Sport Joys

and

Gifts of Play

By
Paul T. Owens

Published by
Myron Publishers
4625 Saltillo St.
Woodland Hills, CA 91364
www.myronpublishers.com
www.paultowens.com

ISBN: 978-0-9824675-0-3
Library of Congress Control Number: 2009928757
Printed in the USA

This book is available for purchase in bulk by organizations and
institutions at special discounts. Please direct your inquiries to
sales@MyronPublishers.com

Cover & Interior Design, Typesetting by Lyn Adelstein.

What People Are Saying About *Sport Joys and Gifts of Play*

"… a prism through which one can glimpse the marrow of an athlete's soul."
>   —*Harold Connolly, 1956 Olympic Gold Medalist,*
>   *Four-time Olympian*

"A most moving experience. A chance to look at and feel the competition, excitement, and pain of athletic endeavor from the very special perspective of poetry."
>   —*Merlin Olsen, Pro Football Hall of Fame,*
>   *All-Pro Defensive Lineman, Los Angeles Rams*

"With his poetic expertise and sensitive insights, Paul T. Owens has captured the elusive answers and descriptions sought by those of us who for so many years have attempted to define our existence as athletes and explain our participation in competitive sports."
>   —*Kate Schmidt, 1972 and 1976 Olympic Bronze*
>   *Medalist, World Record Holder Women's Javelin,*
>   *Three-time Olympian*

About Paul T. Owens

As a sports writer, Paul T. Owens has written for the New York Times and the Los Angeles Times. He was coaching staff writer for the Dallas Cowboys with Tom Landry, and Senior Staff Writer with the 1984 Los Angeles Olympic Committee for Peter V. Ueberroth. He also served as Public Service Coordinator for the United States Olympic Committee.

Paul wrote biographies of National Football League officials and coaches, and for the Victor Awards, one of the longest running sports awards television shows.

He is the author of several other books, which appear on his website: www.PaulTOwens.com.

Mr. Owens received his bachelors and masters degree in business from the University of Southern California, and attended Columbia University Writer's Program.

Stanley Silver, Fine Artist

Stanley Silver earned his Bachelor of Fine Arts at the University of Arizona in 1991, and continued his education at the Art Center in Pasadena. A master of the unforgiving medium of watercolor, as well as a highly developed oil painter, Silver uses both mediums to create a dramatic and timeless feel in all of his work. His art has been shown at some of the most prominent galleries and museums in the United States. His work has also been named the "official art" for many of sports' most prestigious events including the World Series, NHL All-Star Game, and New York Marathon.

Dedication

This book is written for people who find fun at play, those who must have games and teams to follow, and those who believe that athletic motion is what keeps the earth moving through space.

*Joe Di Maggio and author Paul T. Owens, 1991 Victor Awards
Honoring the 50th Anniversary of Joe Di Maggio's 1941
56-game hitting streak.*

Table of Contents

Sport Joys and Gifts of Play Poetry   **8**

Olympic Sports 8
Basketball 40
Football 64
Baseball 94

Words of Sport   **110**

Articles   **111**

Will a New Pro Football Field Really Look Like This? 113
America's Greatest Athlete Plays his Games at Home 115
What Can be Done with Athletic Wastelands? 118
Don't Trade Players, Trade Whole Team 122
Super Bowl—Played At Home and Away 125
Honesty and Speed Will Win More than Games 126
Second Place: the Dreaded Medal 128
Basketball Must Take a Shot at the Future 132
Protect Your Local Quarterback 135
And Now a Few Vital Statistics About the Sport Fan 138
Sport Sounds That Can Heal 141
Some Loopholes for the Overtaxed Sports Fan 144

Mitch Gaylord
Olympic Champion — 1984 Los Angeles Olympic Games
Gymnastics

I am the Olympic Games—the poetic grandeur of play.

I define myself in the context of how I move, which way I go,
and how each movement is an element of beauty—
for I am a participant in beauty, offering you a vision of my reach
to design grace in an effortless and constant way,
and it is not I who moves, but beauty who has found a way
of unfolding itself through me. I am only here to be taken.

I am the Olympic Games—
I reach out for the space in the distances where all thoughts to excel
join together and fly with the strength of the labors of Hercules,
declaring infinitely across the universe
that this my body is.

I am the Olympic Games,
gathered from all lands
to celebrate the gifts of struggle of
each man and woman
to expand the physical possibilities of themselves.
I come to excite the imagination,
to make harmony of the extreme natures of man
and prove that the earth moves only
according to the quality of life at play.

Official Report—1984 Los Angeles Olympic Games
Paul T. Owens

If you saw him or her gliding right out in the air
between two buildings,
you would think it's just where they belong—
natural that the air could hold them so easily.
They move not just for a gymnastic showcase
in an auditorium
with high electric lights
and wild enthusiastic crowds,
but to show us rhythms we can walk in
when we take ourselves from one place
to another.

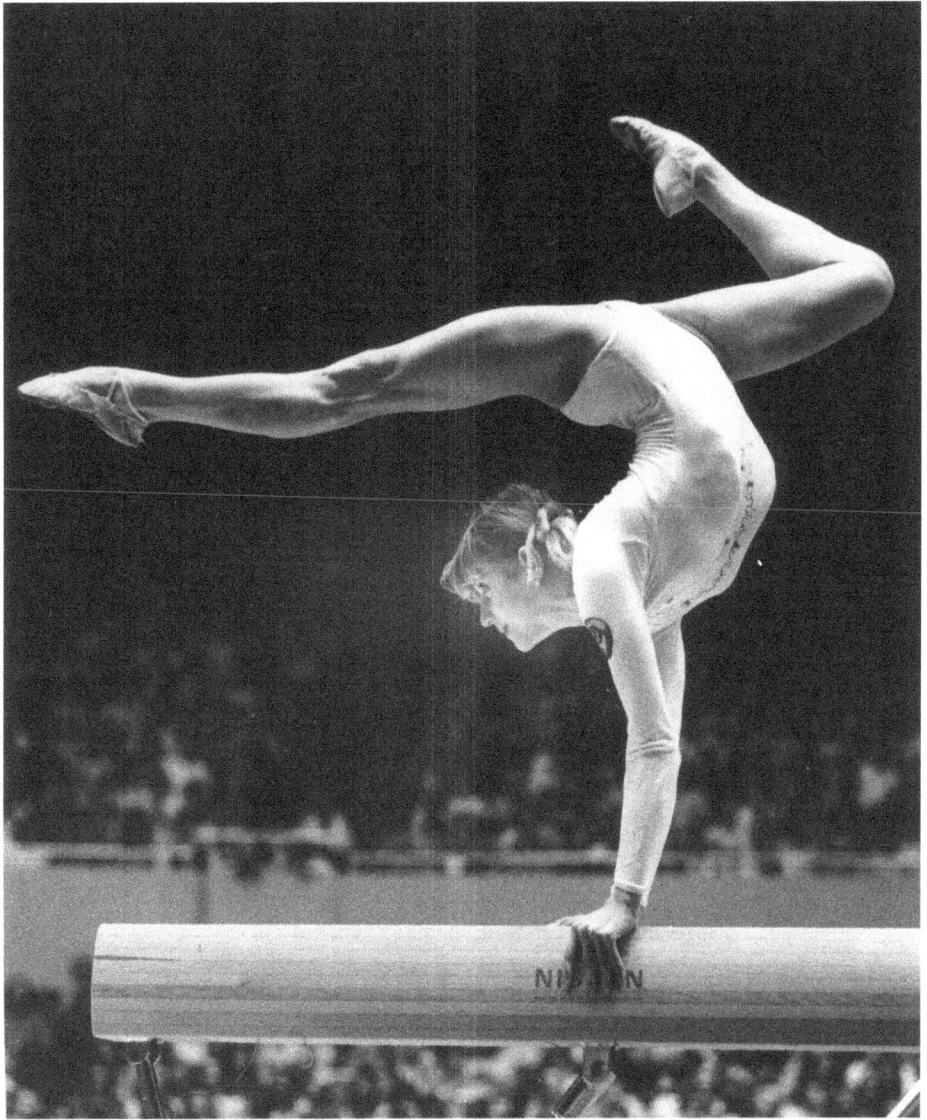

Olga Korbut
Three-Time Gold Medalist
1972 Munich Olympic Games
Gymnastics

And who was the greatest athlete,
who had the most talent,
and whose accomplishments
had been appreciated the most.

All the athletes,
all of them—
those who were just learning games
of play
and those who had long dominated games of sport—
all of them gathered to
decide

and they found
after speaking of the greatest
athletic courage,
magic
and surprise
that the only greatness
all of them could claim
was how well they kept themselves
within the first and most
basic instinct—the need to move.

The extreme natures of man
can be brought together
through the discipline of athletics—
that middle sense of life
that touches the slow, evolving, common ground
of growing gentleness.

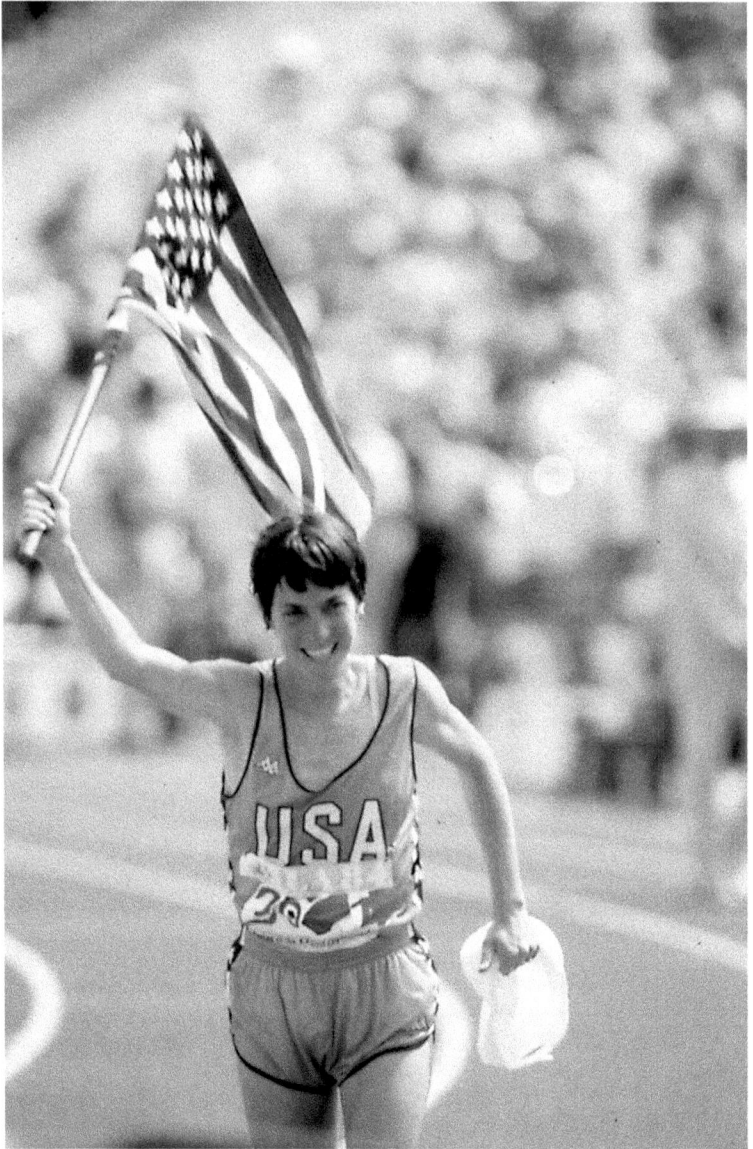

Joan Benoit, Gold Medalist
1984 Los Angeles Olympic Games
Women's Marathon

You said you would win,
that there wasn't much of a chance for me
if you were in the race,

> And I said nothing;
> I just listened.

And then you said how you would win,
how everyone else would follow,

> And I said nothing;
> I just listened.

> I was impressed,
> though, with your confidence.
> I had never met anyone
> who was so sure.
> I did not realize how strong
> your words and ideas were

Until I passed you during the race,
and all of your energies,
your intentions and ideas,
poured out of you and into me.

Francie Larrieu,
Olympian

I am running
and want to go faster
and tell myself, "Yes! Now!"
and it happens ...

And soon I am deep into the sound
of my body fading away,
unaware of where my body ends
and the rest of the world begins.
My memory seeps back into time
to where I first believed
that no one could catch me ...

And my face spreads in a smile,
for I have found
what I thought I had forgotten—
I want to run
forever.

Steve Prefontaine
Olympian

They warned him not to run so often,
that he was not ready for the fast terms
and long-winded runs he was going through.

He told them he had to continue going,
the urge to run hidden so deeply
and surfacing so suddenly he could not stop

that all of his life he had spent on words, thoughts,
ideas, and a total over-intellectualization of life
and now he had to let his body and mind act as one
and do exactly as he wanted

which was to run
from one race to another
connecting all runners
keeping himself further and further
away from the last fraction of a second
that refuses to happen.

The veins in my arms—
those rivers on my skin—
the flowing strength of my body
winding the world around.
I am earth.
I breathe, and mountains rise.
My wrist turns, and a dance comes
out of the wind.
My hands open and close.
A flower I grow.
I am earth.
I spin in an orbit from the spirit
flowing through me, and the
stars move, so I know I cannot stop.
I am trees that fold in abstract
directions.
Progress! Forward!
My arms design the sky.
My legs run to balance where
I came to go again, and
I carry the world bouncing
galaxies off each other.
I find nowhere I go
where I am not already.
Up and out, I take a giving message
that reaches out to make me everyone!

You can't have both
you can't splash through the water
and expect to find your footprints
when the water has slipped away.

You can't outrun a wave
for each has no end in time
but you can always be the pace
the hard wet sand is passed
beneath you to those who
follow.

1984 Olympics
Women's Marathon

The furthest image is how far you see yourself
going on long after the race is finished,
long after someone
has told you how fast you ran,
how many people were ahead or
behind you.
Long after you have rested,
your mind is still not convinced of your
body's conclusion
and goes on
to find your distance
at the end of the running earth,

for you, the long-distance runner,
move on at the speed of a dream that will appear
millions of years from now when the echo of your
feet pounding the earth
is heard again
as it was when you ran on this path
before as a deer, a gazelle
and a lion ...

Dwight Stones
Three-time Olympian
Ten-time World Record holder

You've got to be able to see yourself
going over the bar
before you can really do it.

You've got to envision yourself going over
before you can feel the bird in you
want to lift you over.

Your strength is your speed
and the explosion when you leave
the ground
is the greatest joy
in being a jumper—
more so than knowing,

   "Can anyone else go as high?"

   and

   "How high can I really go?"

And as you ready to jump higher
than anyone else in recorded history,
with all the confidence you have
and all the enthusiasm the world
feels for your success,
you want to hear a voice,
an idea
or word of doubt
that you may have heard
when you first jumped,
someone saying,
"No, you can't make it."

A sound to challenge
the positive silence
you have made with the bar
so that your jump now
will be just as your first
jump
when you had no idea if you
would make it.

The discus thrower—
the lover of the wind,
breathes in the cheering energy of life on earth,
listens for the strength of the winds that carry well,
then turns to the sky to the gods
who have enlarged the world forever,
and sends the word to the power of all infinities.

Within a weightless ounce of time, shot putter,
you have measured space;
and in your spinning circle of thrust
reach out for a wider opening of the universe.

John Naber
Four-Time Olympic Gold Medalist, One-Time Silver Medalist
1976 Montreal Olympic Games

I want to swim far enough
to hear
the ends of the universe
tell where
the next oceans
will spill out of the sky
and design
the final moving infinitive
to swim in.

I want to swim fast enough
to marvel at how each
wave
holds one more stroke
to make my last
seem so much farther
and farther away,

and I want to know
what is as pure as a truth
so constant
its straightness
is absolute,
as sure as
one stroke
keeps giving itself
to another.

Beach Volleyball

Seeing the prayer-shaped angles
she makes of her arms
as she taps the volleyball up

to heights that vary
like the sun
reaching across the ocean,

the constant beginnings
of her feet on dry sand
on days given for jumping:

we know
she will always be
part of the promise
to keep the sky and earth
moving together.

Climbing out of a twist
abandoned upward
cosmic hands reach down
to guide me
to where
I will be one of the lights
that has danced out of its own
image
and one step closer to the final question,
        How high can I reach?

Icarus! Son of Daedalus,
who wore wings made of feathers
to escape into the sky!
You, Icarus—
lover of the happiness of soaring heights—
have given dreams
to vaulters and jumpers of today,
dreams of leaping from mountains,
dreams of falling out of mystical clouds.
You, Icarus—
glider of time—
would be with us today,
had not the sun
melted the wax
that held your wings aloft.

And Icarus had a sister,
Lydeon,
who early in life
climbed upon the rays of the sun
and chose to live among
the stars and planets
in constant fluid motion.

Victory Ceremony
1984 Los Angeles Olympic Games

If there must be one purpose
for why I play,
let it be that
I am given the chance
to be part of a concept that is bigger
than myself—
something that works according
to the trust
each human element has in the other—
an idea that is going after what
will make of the whole bigger parts ...

Basketball is the dance of floating rhythm
to the music
of a bouncing chord,
and the rhythm of millions
of bouncing basketballs
has given the earth its pulse,
and is now ready
to challenge the planets
for the perfection
of all moving spheres.

Eulogy for Basketball Coach Cale Newcomer
Skyline College, San Francisco, California

The two young sisters stood on top of a hill near their home and wondered about the sun and the moon.

The oldest said, "Did you know that the moon was once a very small ball and when no one wanted to play with it, it made itself bigger and went away. And did you know that the sun once was very small also, and when everyone played with it so much it got so hot that it had to fly away?"

"And now they are all by themselves?" her sister asked.

"Yes, they are; but they throw darkness and light to each other every day."

Daughters of Sim and Cale Newcomer,
Tora and Molly

I am jumping and shooting outside
on the stones and dirt,
and someone hears me and comes out to play.
And when others come, there isn't enough room,
so we go to a bigger place and begin playing more,
and become good.
Then others come to watch us,
so we move inside,
where there are polished wooden floors to play on
and lots of people
watching.

Of Jerry West
University of West Virginia
Los Angeles Lakers

The player who played against me
was really working with me.
He caused me to make moves
I had never made before,
and any magic that came
from the surprise of what I did
came because he guarded me so well.

The two of us
were just working together,
creating a new form
to get to the same place.

Of Gail Goodrich, UCLA
Teammate Jerry West
Los Angeles Lakers

44

Backboards hang down from the sky,
their circles an iron-rimmed eye,
all open to the stuffing in
of every kind of leaping grin.

And working out in our squeaking shoes,
we design more joy for the jumping news.
As all cheering voices do resound,
we sky for beauty, and as a beast rebound.

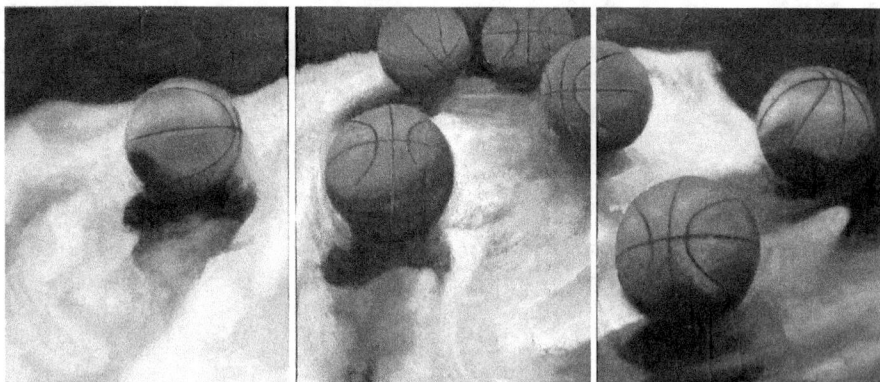

Of Bill Russell,
Boston Celtics
Wilt Chamberlain,
Los Angeles Lakers

He went to those who had won and won often
and asked them what it was that had made them do so well

and they answered

and he followed everything they said but could
not win and returned to them to ask why

and they told him he should listen more to his
own instincts than trying to play like someone else

and he wanted to know how they listened so well

and they told him by not going to others and asking them
how to win, to stop putting so much importance on winning
and just try to have a good time

and he asked them when the good time for them began
and they said, "When we started to win and win often."

Wilt Chamberlain
Los Angeles Lakers

It's not how many times the ball goes into the basket
but how it spins around the rim,
teasing us that it might not go in at all.

It's not how many times, but did it snap the
bottom of the net as it went quickly through?

It's not how many points we score
but how amazed we can be when the ball went through
when we thought there wasn't a chance it would,
or that it didn't when we knew for sure
it should have.

And can we ever jump high enough
to follow the ball,
spin around the rim after it, over
and around again
and then down through the basket to raise
the world two points higher?

It is not to go inside and hide,
playing away from the natural elements
on an evenly measured in-and-out-of-bounds
floor
of a heated gym ...
No, that's not it at all ...

It is to go out
and take on the rain
as fast streaking dribbles that bounce
only once
as you try to find your way
around rocks and open asphalt
slow and subtle pools in streets of
mud roadways
guessing where and if the
ball will bounce its way
back to your wet slapping
hand touch.

Changing lights—sun to moon—night break
Laguna Beach, California

The game is played to find who will take the last shot,
the one right before the light is squeezed out of the sky
and the players stop to watch the moon dribbled behind the
back of night and shot through the basket of dawn.

They just go back and forth—
they don't go anywhere
they don't get anywhere—

but it's exciting when they jump and grab the ball
out of the air before it comes down on its own,
and make moves that often surprise us.

There is grace in their bodies,
the speed they make is real,
but where are they going and
will they get there soon?

Basketball Court, Columbia University,
New York, New York

No one would choose him to play.
They said he wasn't good enough,
that he would make either team he played on lose.
He said he had as much right to play as anybody else
and, besides, "I am your friend."
And they said, "No,"
and he said, "Why don't we take turns being the one
who stands around and watches the game?"
And they said, "No, go play by yourself."

He came back again and again to ask to play
and they said, "No," every time.

And then he didn't ask anymore, but went to play alone.
Soon he was able to play better than all of them and they
came to him and said, "We want you to play with us."

He just shook his head, "No."

"We want you to play on our team," one player said.
"No, we want him on ours," another spoke.

He just shook his head, "No."

"That's not right. What good does it do if you don't play?"
another player asked, and he said, "It wouldn't be fair. Either
team I played on would win."

Field House
University of Detroit,
Detroit, Michigan

right after the game
after everyone had left
he came back to the court
and made the shot
he missed at the end of the game,
the shot
everyone thought was
the one that decided the game,
which he did not feel was true
for every shot made or missed
could have been the one that separated the winners
from the losers
it did not have to be his ...

and he made the shot over and over again
so many times that he did not believe he ever
missed it during the game,
and when people reminded
him
the next day
the next week
the next year
how they had seen him miss
that one shot
he asked them
why they did not stay after the game
to see how many times he made it.

Larry Hollyfield, UCLA

It's not enough for it just to be what it was;

we have a need for art to remember,
to make it appear faster than it did,
a higher level of beauty through an added visual image,
something that will prevail

so we can wait for someone to tell us when they see it,
"I was there and didn't even see that."

Big yellow red moon
dropping,
by the time I get to where you land
when you fall out of the sky
will you be small enough for me to
catch
and can you stay long enough for me
to try to put you through
all the baskets on all the backboards—

or will I have to throw you back
          into the sky
                because you are just a rebound
                    that players
                      from another world
                        are coming to get?

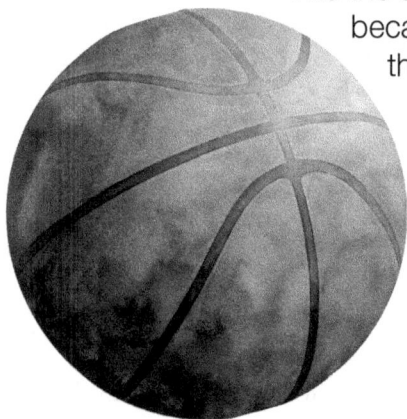

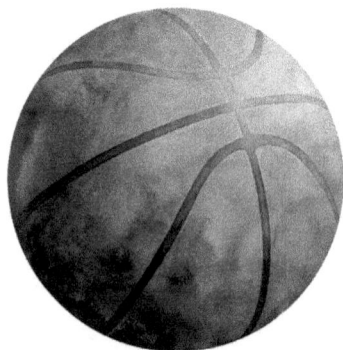

Show me a dribbler
who is scrambled in speed so quickening
through
the whirling
flying
jumping personalities
about him that no one knows
no one really knows
if he is controlling
the ball
or the ball
is controlling him
as he spins in
and around
over and up
to the basket

Shhhhhh ...
Quiet ...

I am trying to hear ...

the sounds of a tired asphalt
blacktop
after a night of
holding up
the bouncing spirits
of streetlight playing
basketball.

Shhhhhh ...

I am trying to hear ...

the sound of a father
telling his son
that it's all right
no matter that he dropped
the ball that was hit
to his field
and the winning run
rounded second and third
and headed for home
and the rest of the world stood and
pointed to the father and the son
to blame them
for making them.

The bouncing
and shooting of basketballs
from polished wooden floors
are the exact same
movement
of all
unknown
and
unseen
universes.

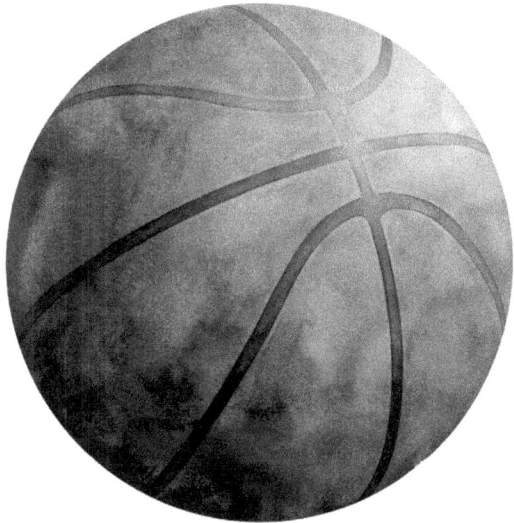

While a seven-year-old boy
concentrates outside alone
imagining millions of people will
be watching his next shot
and he will be his own hero

a player in a game watched
by millions tries to make believe
he is outside alone
with no one watching.

Out of the corner stand the starting five,
hunched in curiosity over what keeps them alive.
They've got the latest pictures
and all the gum they can chew
and are trading cardboard faces of their players
old and new.

And so smart they think themselves with all of their trades,
their parents want to know
if they can "trade in" some of their grades.
But perhaps if they know so much
about each game and every score,
colleges will offer them scholarships
for how they can learn much more.

Beverly Hills High School
Swim Gym
December Basketball Tournament

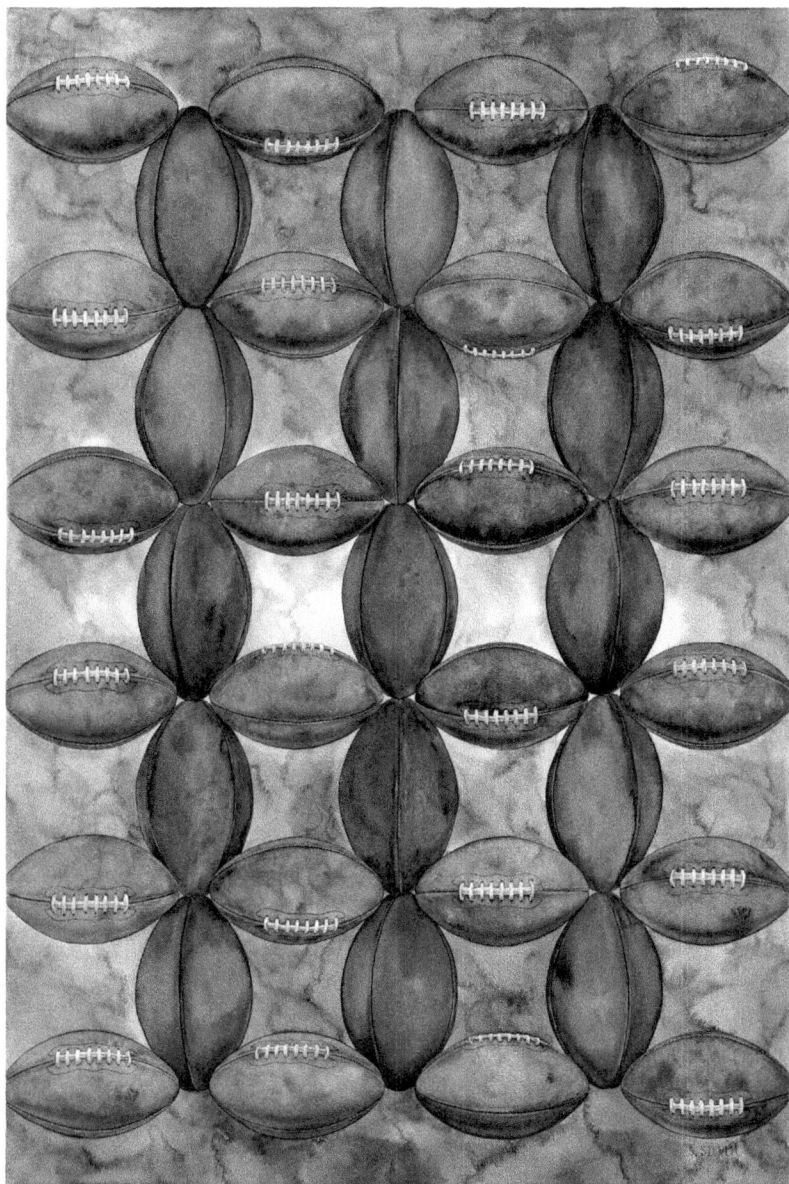

Stickers on the window
banners on the door
everyone's gotta know
who we're rooting for.

Names on sitting blankets
inscriptions on the walls
all stand up for our team
and cheer the loudest calls.

We're No. 1! We're No. 1!
What else would you want to be
than the All-American spirit of
a winning season and your Ph.D.

❧

I saw a man draw pictures of children playing
in the fields, kicking a ball to and away from each other;
talking to a woman who was imagining
what new geometric form there would be
if she took all the lines made of their kicking
and connected them with string and watched it
fly away ...

and then I went to the city and heard a man
who had designed tall buildings made of concrete and steel,
wood and glass, speak of how the lines
of a building do not stand high and strong as a result of the
strength of the structure or design of the architecture or the
temperament of the earth,
but rather by the quality of life
of the children who played about them ...

and then I went to the arena
and heard the unanimous cry of the crowd
name the fifty-yard line of the football field
as the longest of all lines, because it has taken in the attention
of millions for thousands of hours,
disguising itself as the center of the universe
and allowing to cross it the longest distance between two
points—the closest score that peacefully separates two
teams who've played
against each other all day.

I feel the sweat of my body's approval,
the adrenaline flowing
in between hope
and despairing unknown.
All seems so possible,
yet so soon can be taken away.
My head hangs loosely limp
across my chest.
I want the waiting
                to stop!
and every thought
                to cease!
I want
to start playing
and be lost in finding out.

"What a catch!"

   "God, what a catch!"

"What a play!"

   "Did you see that?"

are the crying voices
of the new earth
of divine revelation
before the stained-glass window of television
on a tucked-in Sunday

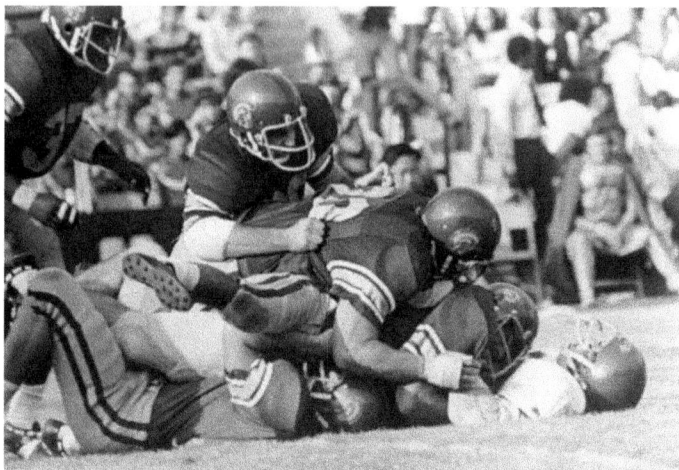

Motion Stoppage—No more yards gained
University of Southern California

I tried squeezing a poem out of a tackle
and got caught between the hands
of the beauty I found.
Flat on my back I saw pictures I wanted to complete.

I wanted to know, where was the
biggest kid who
ever got away from having to play
on the front line
against the other team's
biggest kid?

Could he tell me where to go to find
one million of the lightest and smallest players
who'd put themselves together
just to be big enough to take his place?

I wanted someone to show me five men
hanging onto a breakaway runner for twenty yards,
so I could paint every bottle of beer that swims across
the chest of America's afternoon
trying to show how it was done.

I wanted the design of a running play
that would have a hundred thousand fans
marching down onto the field, right to the goal line.
And I wanted to see a dance
that Bach's harpsichord would play gloriously to the crowd,

And as I looked up,
I wondered where the sounds of compassion were
stored—those oohs and aahs for the man
who got cut down by a pile of men,
for I wanted to be part of a safer fantasy
that is slow enough to have a hug in it for everyone,
to have smiles that don't get lost in the shuffle
while falling to the ground.

No matter your talent
and the intentions you have of catching the ball,
to take it out of the air
and say "I got it,"
it only comes to your hands to stay if it wants
to ...

You may find it and lose it in the sun
and overhanging electrical lights,
twist your legs about you,
stumble, fall, get up and chase after it again,
but if it doesn't want to be caught—
whatever its reasons—
it won't be,
and when you pick it up and scream how it was almost yours,
how you had it for sure,
all you can be certain of is that it wouldn't
and couldn't be caught this time....

Go ahead!
Put twenty-five cents of mustard
on twenty-five cents of relish
on twenty-five cents of onions
and have them running together
on a twenty-five-cent hot dog
that's not twenty-five cents anymore,
and see if it tastes the same in your living room
as it does after you've run from the vendor
underneath the stadium's sloping arches,
dropping your mustard,
onions, and relish
over the edges
just in time
to stand for the kickoff.

Seymour, sons and daughter
—the race to the kick-off.
Los Angeles Coliseum

The end of a plastic-covered line
fits into the ear of a man
who sits watching the opera Aida.
The line is attached to a radio
in his inside coat pocket;
the radio is turned to the voice of a sportscaster
who is calling the plays of the game
four-thousand miles away
from where the man is holding hands with his wife,
and smiling as the opera moves on.

As the quarterback
in the team dressing room
puts eyeliner
beneath his eyes
to help keep the sun out
when he plays,

a cheerleader
blooms before the mirror
in her sorority dressing room,
painting her face
in fluid peach and cherry,
blending her lips
in a burgundy line,
she brushes her hair
into a flapping-smile flip and jumps
to articulate the facts of the afternoon,

"I look delicious, and we're gonna win."

Cheerleader
University of Nebraska
2000

73

I have seen and heard every football stadium filled with
the colors of the roaring greed that must win and win forever.

I have listened to the stories of the greatest wisdom
ever told and am convinced the greatest teller is the
one who knows who will win and by how much.

And I have just heard that the greatest play has just been made again,
this time before the largest audience ever assembled in
the remotest of all watching lands and spaces

as up the numbers go
to the most important athletic numbers—
those that compare what we have done in sports
to what we have done in space;

how far we have traveled through the galaxies in one try—one look—
with how far we have thrown and jumped on earth,
fractions of inches to billions of miles,

how fast we can run to how swift we have traversed the
mysteries of the cosmos,
the quickest sprinting stride to the fastest
thought that does wonder.

Running Against Oblivion

How long before all original parts have to be replaced
and his speed runs out of time and
his gift to deceive with his dancing steps is
only a blur in his quest to
never be forgotten.

The greatest moment in his career,
as one of the greatest football runners,
wasn't in scoring the most touchdowns in one game,
nor running the most yards in one game
one season
one decade,
nor making the longest run
or the longest catch,
nor was it when he stood before the country
at festive banquets given in his honor.

No,
none of the list of apparent successes,
he said, could match the time
when he walked by a playground, unnoticed,
and heard a young boy call out to his friends
that he was him
as he tucked the ball in at his side,
ran with it,
and yelled back to his friends,
"You can't catch me, I'm ..."

Although he was the biggest and strongest on the team,
he was too gentle and too kind
to play with any VICIOUSNESS.
So it was decided
        by the team,
        the coach,
        and the people who came to see him play
that he should spend some time
        in a cage
        with wild animals
to develop a greater need
        for AGGRESSION
        and RAGE.

But everyone was disappointed,
for when they threw open the cage
to let him out,
the animals walked out
gently and tamely
by his side.

The girls said they would play with the boys if they would not hit them like they hit each other
and the boys said they would play with the girls if they would not use the rough words the boys used when they pushed each other around
and the girls said no, 'cause they knew football was not just running with a ball and knocking people down, it was words, hard words
and the boys said all right,
but the girls wanted to know if their best player could play,
and the boys said sure, anyone you want can play
and the girls told them that they would be sorry because she scores on every play,
which the boys laughed at, we got to see this,
they said, bring her around, we'll get her every time, and she came
and they never caught her, which made one boy post a warning on all the trees in the parks wherever she played,

"You can chase her far and fast,
and promise your heart that it will last,
but she is the touchdown lady, my friend,
and a broken heart is how you'll bend."

De Neve Park,
Los Angeles, California

I wonder all the games
the bottles and cans hold
as they stand on the shelves waiting
to be taken and poured
down cheering
dry throats

how many games in each bottle
how many winning shouts squeezed into
each can
how smooth and fast
all fun is swallowed.

It seems that a brutal,
primitive inspiration
and a total disregard for the body
are the incentives
for these flying angles
to wildly collapse around each other.

But it is not true,
for what is there
is an intentional force,
pursued in the midst of concentration,
a mere guess for space
in a vacuum of time,
feeling for balance
within the unknown, possible motions
of constant change, as

I take the players
coming from all points to bring me down
and turn them
into the magic finds
of my own direction;
so sure am I
that their strength, size, and number
are only symbols
to confuse my concentration.

82

the pictures
the pennant
the programs
the pens

the hats
the T-shirts
of the heroes
and friends

the autograph
the thin line
of fast-written ink

scribbles a memory
to dream of
and think

of when we'll go back
to the stadium
for more of the same

but, dad, I know,
I am the only hero
you can ever name.

I've seen the anxious and spirited
heart of the blonde streak of a Southern belle
wave and scream GO TEAM
DEFENSE—OFFENSE—
as she marched into the hell-raising
ringing warmth
of a victory autumn night.

I've seen every thermos bottle couple
laugh their beer into tears
at every weekend game
since college made Saturday
sacred

and have watched games from TV rooms
filled with exhausted men
who earn each play, emotionally
rising to the drama of the moment
of crisis
with high volume second-guessing,
their laps full of bets and point spreads
their heads with the latest conviction
that wisdom is the man
with the foresight to know who's going to win
and by how much.

I've heard the men on the radio and television
enthuse and have read the exaggeration
of those whose purpose is
to create a section for sports in a city's
newspaper
and I am convinced their words
have swelled our fantasies
into myths of greatness
because we've wanted to believe
football-watching is all that we
can have

and that we are in the midst of the
era of the greatest plays of all time
which can only be outdone by the
regrouping of all greatness
when the greatest catch
has just been caught again
this time by the most overrated

superstar man-child
who ever played under the tutelage
of the winningest
coach who ever had the decency
not to treat his men
as animals
but as the highest-ranking soldiers
who ever marched off to war

I've multiplied all those who've watched
every game
by the multitude of emotions spent
by the hours played
and have found this to be
the highest amount of intensity and interest ever,
higher than all the wonder spent on learning
and creating,

for higher than everything else
is the uninterrupted line
that connects the winner and loser
and the longest distance between two points
is the closest score that separates two teams
on the same field.

The Color of Orange
University of Tennessee

We build stadiums
        to yell
        to scream
and snuglysittogether
and rise as one
hysterically
        when things
        are getting
better.

The team we love
        to win
        to lose
is only secondary;
        to let the gods
        know
we're still alive
        is the reason
primary.

Saturday morning sunup,
to the school for the college soccer game,
the afternoon is for football, the crosstown
rivalry is untamed;
at nightfall to the hockey arena to yell as fast
as the moving puck,
and if no heart attack by midnight, then we've
had all the luck.
But it's straight up for Sunday to sit and meditate
on why a deep religion
should regulate our fate.

In wrapped and padded shorts and pants
a scampering quarterback does his dance,
away from the sudden and anxious hands
of those who now come rushing to change his plans.
The quarterback twists and turns out of their way
not just for his team or his own glory to play,
but for the millions who've bet the odds to be able
to put money in their pockets and food on their table.

I'm the happy rooter 'cause my team's the winning one;
I won't cheer for any loser, 'cause that wouldn't be much fun.
I know that I'm quite fickle, 'cause I cheer on every play,
but I am just for the team that's doing well,
and that's where my allegiance will stay.

I'd rather root for the good play and those who are doing best
than be upset for having favorites who aren't playing like the rest.
I don't care for any home team unless they're way ahead,
and when the visitors take the lead, I cheer for them instead.

I am the happy rooter 'cause my team's the winning one;
I won't cheer for any loser, 'cause that wouldn't be much fun.

In their restaurant by the harbor,
John cooks the fish his brother catches
and business is usually good, for they are
nice and not cheap with the fish,
they work six days a week—
8 in the morning 'til 10 at night and on Tuesdays sleep
all day and once a month go to the movies with
their friends.
The money they make doesn't go to drinking
or for the trip they often speak of;
no, the money passes from the tourists, the locals
through the sweat of John and his cramped
kitchen crew's wet hands,
the heat broiling fish, slices of lemon, garlic, and butter,
seasonings of pepper,
to a man who comes every afternoon at 3
ever since the restaurant was opened,
for waging on how well the business of men who
play sports against each other will do, men
neither John nor his brother know or see on television
or listen to on radio or go to the stadium to see—
all of their money given to the success of hunches,
an entire everyday fascination with chance,
the surety of the heat and fish, garlic, and lemons,
seasoning offerings
to the world,
balanced by the challenge of the magic
to one day guess all scores.

Gloucester, Massachusetts

In the way of verbal abuse,
refs get more than they can use;
trying to keep everything clean and right,
a hatred in everyone they ignite.

These running policemen rush on by
to make sure ball-stealing robberies are not done on the sly.
They make all of us humans decry the human element,
for we don't excuse their mistakes and won't let them repent.

Of John McDonough
National Football League
Super Bowl IV Referee

Throw me a feeling that won't go anywhere but in the basket.

Give me a thought that is as perfect as a pass
that slips beyond the grasp of all defenders,
right into the fingertip-waiting hands of the
intended receiver.

And find me a fantasy
that appears so real
that when we move towards it
it is taken away,
just as a curve ball we swing at
breaks away from us as it
crosses the plate
leaving us nothing.

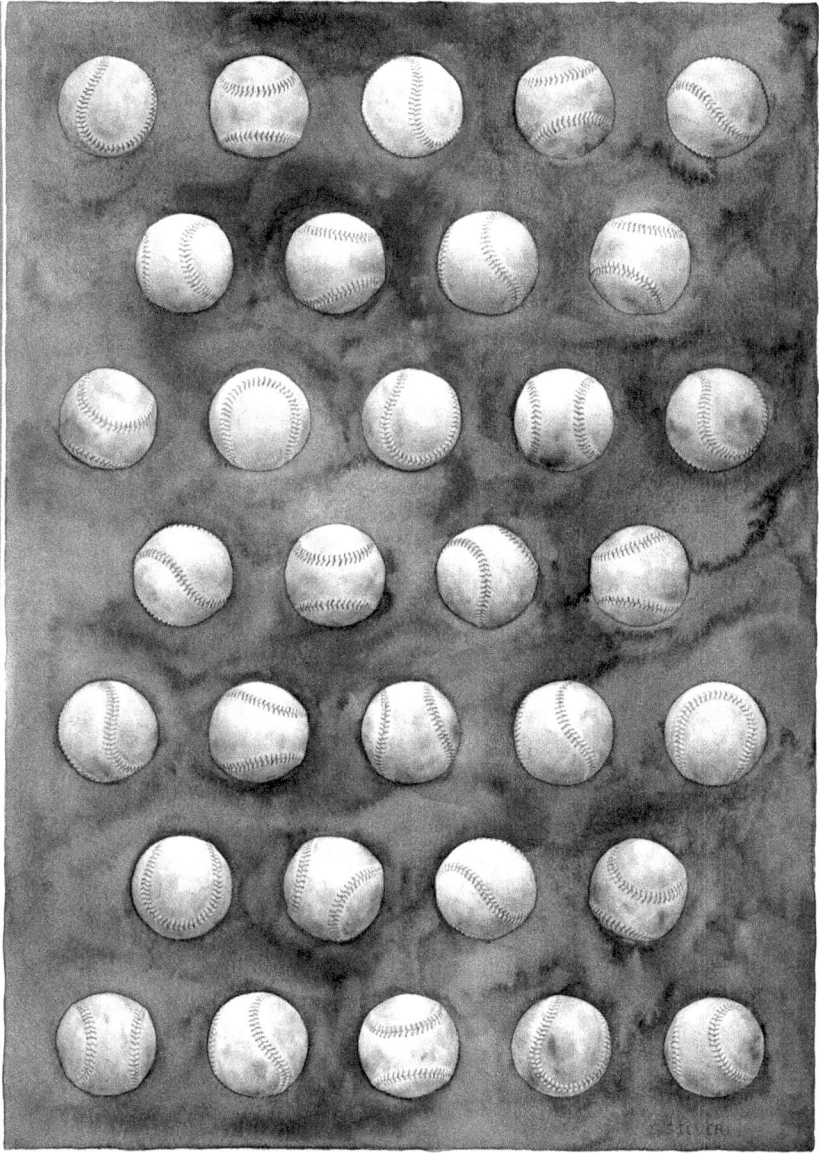

Baseball is the story of a line and a circle,
the swinging sides of angles
made of a soft Saturday's
grass and sand.

I am the beholder of anticipation
and offer myself and every batter I face
the challenge to increase
our perception of time, space,
and the control of our energy.

So close to their playing
we could see everything in their faces.
So close, we could.

And the dirt-worn, green wood grandstands
would bend with our stomping feet.
All of us so close together—
they were playing as if in our own backyard.
We could feel and yell everything
until the machines came
to tear down and rebuild,
to let more people in,
and make our view wider and longer,
and take the coziness
out of our fun.

The longest
hit is
the one
that can't be seen—
the one that is hit so far,
so hard that
we have no idea
where it will land,
or if it ever will;
that is the hope,
the reason we come.
That is why we
can sit so
quietly,
waiting
so long.

And when it is hit,
we can rise as one,
hysterically,
to celebrate the possibility
of this being
the infinite inning,
when the hit no one can catch
climbs over the
farthest fielders'
outstretched hands—
on up through
our fantasies, to find a way
we can follow.

If I take every positive
and beautiful purpose
and multiply it
for a year
by everyone
who feels its spirit,
will the reverberations
survive
the roaring chant
of the crying crowd
to win and
win forever?

way out in the outfield
     in between left and center

         two boys
       chased a ball
    that was coming down
  through the rays of the sun
and as they both jumped to catch it

  it   dropped
       in
    between
    them

    and
theyknockedintoeachother
      a
      n
      d

      f
      e
      l
      l

    to the ground . . .

and the people in their families
     yelled   at each other
      that   the   other
        child   was   to
          blame

   as the boys lay on the ground
   and the winning runs
   rounded second and third
   and headed for home.

throw it hard, jimmy, jimmy, throw it hard,
you're the greatest, jimmy

but NOT SO HIGH, jimmy pitch it to his glove,
come on jimmy, pitch it to his glove

not so high jimmy, that's too high the ump wants a strike,
jimmy you gotta throw them strikes

down, jimmy that a boy, jimmy get 'em down,
jimmy you're the greatest, jimmy
jimmy, you're the greatest

don't walk nobody, jimmy
oh, jimmy, don't walk him, too no, jimmy, no ...

jimmy, you don't even look like a ball player out there,
you know you are—so act like one
pitch like you know how—take your time
you're pushing too hard, jimmy—take it easy, jimmy
but get it up there, jimmy, you gotta, come on ...

please, jimmy, everybody is watching
your father is here and you know he didn't
want you to play and I begged him to let you
and now you're throwing the game away
you're letting us all down maybe he's right, jimmy
you shouldn't be playing on anyone's team
'cause you're a loser but come on, jimmy,

show 'em you're not—show 'em, jimmy
ah, come on, jimmy
don't make me come out to the mound
to take you outta there, come on, jimmy,
control yourself, come on, jimmy, throw it harder,
harder, jimmy, throw it harder, jimmy, come on.

Because the game took 6 hours and 53 minutes,
all of tonight's scheduled shows
had to be cancelled
and a 2-hour analysis
of the game will now follow
superseding the usual time
given to the news
of the latest deaths
and fires and bombs
and suspects wanted
and families separated
in the face of war.

though the game took 6 hours and 53 minutes,
our team is now 10 games ahead of the team
in second place
in the race for the real flag
that says 12 percent of the working force
doesn't want to work
because a constant watch on every game
is more important than raising
the gross national product
and the truest strength of the nation
is the national batting average
with a populace that knows
who's above and below it
with unemployment compensation
paid according to how well
anyone follows the home team
right down the line of summer
'til the last out of the final
game of the season.

because the game took 6 hours and 53 minutes,
every dog's walk has been delayed,
for the leashes of all animal lovers
have been attached to every television channel
world
and all clocks have been set back 3 hours
to give everyone the chance
to rest for tomorrow night's game

and because the game finished
early this morning,
a young boy
has set the American League record
for 6-year-olds staying
up late
and has promised the world
he will pray for the endless inning
with no more midnights
and no more dawns
to ever remind him he has ever slept
or ever has to sleep again.

because the game took 6 hours and 53 minutes,
4 million
682 thousand
324 pages
of books and magazines
went unread and unshared,
and because of the game,
the world's penchant for
its own immobility
has increased threefold.

because the game took 6 hours and 53 minutes,
the Congress for Eternal Peace Among All Nations
has postponed its final decree
until a complete investigation can be made
into the effects of chaos caused
by the drinking of beer on the
mind of the
public crowd ...
and because of the game,
all late liquor laws have
been rescinded so that
beer can flow timelessly
through all games.

because the game took 6 hours and 53 minutes,
the president's speech on human energy
was not shown

but will appear on the last pages of
tomorrow night's program,
the speech that decries the
power of the local fan in support
of the home team to
undermine
the need for brotherhood
and the total spirit of
an undivided union

and because the game took 6 hours and 53 minutes,
we celebrate the coming
of the infinite inning
when the hit no one can catch
climbs
over the farthest fielders'
outstretched hands
and on up through
our fantasies
to imagine how
we can find a
way to follow.

The little league has taken away my son
and blamed him for not hitting every home run.
He's sat on the bench for most of the season,
when he was promised to play, 'cause fun is the reason.

He's ashamed of himself—and who wouldn't be—
every mother calls him a bum 'cause he's 0 for 23.
The uniform he wears, the hat and the spiked shoes,
have given him the glory, but not how to handle how to lose.

He's gone three weeks now without talking to anyone
'cause a hitless summer, he says, isn't his idea of fun.
And though we all tried to give him emotional support,
he says a loser must suffer alone to play the sport.

The Abduction of Matthew Alzer No. 86

In cardboard boxes
plastic cups with
black coffee with cream and sugar
sit next to cokes with ice
next to hot dogs wrapped in
white bread rolls
wrapped in wax paper
under a fast-painted mustard line and
all held together by a fast-climbing
cigar-puffing father who
watches his binocular-carrying son
up the eighty-step stadium
staircase to the top
where they will watch as the game
raises up and down
the drinks and
the hot dogs
inside them.

Numbers,
he's two for three
driven in four
tripled in the second
singled in the fourth
with the count two and one on
him now
with men on
second and third
he looks at the first-base coach
who looks at the third-base coach
who gets the signal from
the manager in the dugout
for how he should hit—
taps the bottom of his shoes with his bat
wiggles his feet to a firm fit
in the ground
puts the bat up above his shoulders
and waits for the ball to come
towards him to finish the swing
that will be one
more strike or ball or hit or foul
of the last innings
of the first game of a
three-game
day-night-morning triple-header.
And the number of people at their wedding
equals the number of hits for his season.

Josh and Laura's marriage
Summer, Santa Monica, California
2009

Guys who say
"Nice guys finish last"
are guys you don't want to be nice to.
Guys who feel that everyone nice
winds up at the end of the line
aren't nice themselves
so they can demand their importance
for not being nice.

And those who don't think
they're ahead or behind
anyone else
look around and wonder when
the guy who thinks he's in front
finds he's merely in the middle
of a bigger line,
a line that no one knows
the end of
or
beginning to
except those who want
to be nice
and believe that everyone is here
first
all at once.

Words of Sport

SPORT---Spectator Play On Remote Television. Games played changing stations to keep a ball always in motion.

BUM---Booing Unmercifully Mistakes.

TELARIDO-When you believe that the athletes you are watching play are doing your cardiovascular exercise for you.

GOAL-Glad Others Are Losing. Your winning tradition continues as long as the teams you do not like lose.

SCREAM---Salary Counting Reduces Everyone's All Around Morale.

TELERCISE--- The belief that the exercises you are doing on your stationery bicycle gives energy to the athletes you are watching on television while you pedal.

FUNGO--- When the fun of a game causes you more pressure than the work you left to play it.

The New York Times

Articles
and
Features

SPORTS

Will a New Pro Football Field Really Look Like This?

By PAUL T. OWENS

The National Football League is ready for a land grab. Not on condominiums in California or lakelands in Florida, or in the cornfields of Kansas, but right down on the fields that take our Sunday energy and give us our tackling thrills.

The football field is ready to go com- companies can use the same space in another stadium the same day.

Firestone may want the 50-yard line and call it the Firestone Fifty. Each week, the middle of the field will be chalked in the design of a tire track. Goodrich, Goodyear, and other tire companies will exchange goal-line tire

The New York Times

SPORTS

WILL A NEW PRO FOOTBALL FIELD
REALLY LOOK LIKE THIS?

The National Football League is ready for a land grab. Not on the condominiums in California or lakelands in Florida or in the cornfields of Kansas, but right down on the fields that take our Sunday energy and give us our tackling thrills.

The football field is perfect for going commercial. No more television viewing being interrupted for sponsored messages. The playing fields need to be subdivided and rented for easy spectator pleasure.

Companies will meet with the League to decide what spaces on the filed will "play" or display their names. The major football industrial complex will be open for bids to fill the surfaces of its colorful playing spectrums.

Instead of it being first and ten, on the 40-yard line it will be first and Pepsi because Pepsi will have paid to rent 10-yards between the 40-and 50-yard line. And if allowed, Pepsi can forbid another bottling company from advertising on the same field. Or, other soft drink and bottling companies can use space at another stadium on the same game day.

Firestone may want the 50-yard line and call it The Firestone Fifty. Each week the middle of the field will be painted or chalked with the picture of tire tracks. Other tire companies will exchange 50-yard line as well as goal-line tire tracks on a game-to-game basis of equal advertising space.

The League will furnish to prospective sponsors facts about

playing time, how much play is done on various areas of the field. For instance, companies will know which teams play good defense at home. Such information can help a sponsor decide which parcels of land it wants to rent when the team plays a weak offensive opponent. Periodic scrutiny will ensure that no team or its players are receiving compensation for playing poorly on one half of the field and not the other.

A sponsoring airline can emblazon the names of the cities it services in the end zone. The team that just scored will turn to the fans and yell out the names of those destinations. Scoring teams will earn a bonus as stipulated by the players' union and the airlines.

The automobile industry will have yardage to advertise its scoring capacity. Each car corporation can post the estimate of how many all-pro miles were driven by fans during the previous week. Compact cars will be pictured facing each other. Each car will wear on its door panels the insignias of one of the teams on the field.

Hero players and hero drinks will be displayed on various divisions of the field. The shaving industry will have before and after shots. An area of a two-foot growth of AstroTurf or grass will designate the before look. Coaches will be urging players to throw it or kick it into the beard area.

Players will have to contend with ads for computer and electronic companies that will blink their logo messages as the players move.

Magazines will show their latest feature covers, and oil companies will show how their products make products work as smoothly as the finely tuned athletes on the field.

And these players will give their all so we can sip the beer they cheer for, ride the planes they score for, and buy the space on our fantasies that show us getting across the goal line first.

114

AMERICA'S GREATEST ATHLETE
PLAYS ALL HIS GAMES AT HOME

The world's greatest athlete might never have scored the winning touchdown, hit the longest home run, or won the trophy for being the most unselfish player on a basketball court.

No, the most talented player is the one at home who can play every game at once, in The Game game—a sport that is still looking to form its own league and hold its first player draft.

All you need to play is a television set or radio when more than one sporting event is being broadcast. The only skills required are good channel hand-eye coordination and hyper-sensitivity to anticipate when the ball will be in play.

The object of The Game game is to keep the ball in motion. A Game player who starts out watching a baseball game will want to change stations as soon as the manager walks out to the mound to talk to his pitcher, right after an out, or at the beginning of the 7th inning stretch.

As soon as the ball becomes dead, the home player is off to another station. If he lands on a tennis match where the players are standing around between sets sipping a Wimbledon tea, he loses a point on his score card. If a player has just hit an overhead slam out of bounds, the home player must quickly switch to another show. If he gets a soccer match while the ball is being kicked around, another point is scored.

The rules of The Game do not allow a player to watch any event longer than two minutes at one time. You can't score points watching a soccer game that goes for an entire period of twenty minutes without a time-out for a foul or goal scored or anything.

You've got to switch to win. Your score is based on how many times you switched and how many times you kept the ball moving. The winner is the one with the fewest stops in the action, in a two-hour game period, having made the minimum amount of switching attempts.

Overlapping sports seasons have helped the sport grow. As many as five games at one time can be included for The Game game competitor—the athlete who has chosen to display his sports instincts and intuition without the aggravation of exaggerated physical play and sweat. There is competition, however, for the players who want to put the "run" in their game. Players who prefer to be switch hitters can run from one room to another trying to keep the action going on more than one set at a time. The point of difficulty will be considered so that the player with one set can compete against the high roller who has to climb stairs to get from one "field" to another. The multi-set player won't have to make as many hits as the player with one set, but his accuracy percentage must be better for him to win.

Competitors don't have to focus on current games. For those who don't like the constant unknown of where the ball is going, or those who don't like soccer or a football-baseball mixture, there is the option of pre-packaged tapes. A player can play with his favorite sports spectaculars, or the games he feels have the best stop-go action. The 1977 Super Bowl game can be teamed with the third play-off game of the 1981 Stanley Cup and a collection of film clips or last-second game-losing free throws. Home players will be able to review the tapes before playing them to plan quick moving strategy, and will not compete against the current 'Game today' players.

The other division of the league consists of those who have overdosed on their sports-watching diets and have been advised to keep to the slower moving game of connecting T. V. commercial times together. The object will be to keep ads on all the time. Any time a player misses by getting tuned into the action, he loses points.

Any Game game player is allowed to take a break from competition if he is way ahead on points. He can turn to a mystery, catch the news, or balance his western sports intensity by sinking into a low-profile meditative trance.

With the advent of The Game game, neighborhoods will thrive again. One house, one city, one state will go against another, not to mention the heightened intensity when fans of a certain team go against each other and match their best average ball movement totals. No longer will the biggest games be played by athletes on the field. The real winner in American sport will be home trying to avoid living room whiplash and knocking his family down while he connects the completion of a 70-yard touchdown pass-play with a tennis ball thrown up for a serve at a women's tennis match. An unhappy victor can say, "Even though I've just won Wimbledon, the US Open, and the hearts of everyone who wants the youngest kid to beat the best of the ladies, my favorite Game game player was disqualified from his championships when the sets he was playing on got so confused by his quick changings that they crashed.

WHAT CAN BE DONE WITH ATHLETIC WASTELANDS?

In the race to build the biggest athletic space, provide the widest, highest and most ornate sports arena, the sports industry insists on wasting half of its playlands. The unused stadium is a bigger extravagance than extra high salaries or inflated ticket prices, and is a sports oversight that is hurting both owners and fans alike. All that has to be done to eliminate the waste is to start playing every game on both teams' home field or court.

No, not two separate games, played two weeks or two days apart. Nor one football game, tackle; the other, touch. Nor, one with first-string players, the other with the second team. No, just one game played the same day with part of each team at home. For instance, the offense of the Houston Texans will play the Pittsburgh Steelers defensive unit in Houston while the Steelers offense is playing the Texans defense in Houston.

While the game is being played in one stadium, the players and fans in the other stadium will follow the action on a televised electronic screen. When there is a change of possession, the announcement will be made for fans to tighten up their rooting belts for the changeover.

"We now switch you to Houston. Please keep your enthusiasm vocal, as your cheering will be piped into the other stadium."

Playing on both fields will give neither team a home team advantage. With both stadiums open for seating the gate receipts will increase. Concession sales will increase. Barring any scheduling inconvenience for other types of arena events (baseball, circuses, etc.), all of the NFL games could be played right at home. The defense would be home one week, offense the next.

Not only would the local fan be able to attend every game, he would save himself the costs of paying for expensive transportation and accommodations in a hostile city, and eliminate the risk of being thrown out of the stands for waving his or her team banners.

Baseball is definitely ready for the every-game-at-home season. No more would there have to be the perfect all-around player. The age of the offensive and defensive specialist would prevail, as it has in football. Each team would have five designated hitters and nine playing fielders. While the Yankee hitters are scoring against the Red Sox pitching staff, the Boston hitters will be taking swings at New York pitching in New York. At the end of each half inning, the action will switch from one field to the other.

No longer will the utility infielder, known for his grace with the glove, have to sit out most of the season because the starting second baseman, who is error-prone, has to be in the line-up for his batting ability. They could both be contributing to the team effort.

Basketball could go "all courts" with one team playing offense, the other defense. The first and third quarters, the 76ers are playing their offensive unit in Philadelphia against the Los Angeles Lakers defense. The second and fourth quarters, everybody is watching the game in Los Angeles with the Lakers playing their offensive unit against Philadelphia's defense. Anytime the defensive team gets a rebound, their score goes up one point and the ball is given back to the offensive team. Full house seating potential now is doubled.

If players object in management-player negotiations that their shooting egos are suffering, that no one should have to play defense all the time, the game could become a series of two games—one team going against another with their center, one forward and one guard in both arenas. Possibly a half dozen contests could make up the final score. (Two-on-two competitions, free throw contests, slam dunk judgings and the number of rebounds, etc.)

No matter the combination, there would be no way fans could suffer because their team is out of town. More sports dollars would be spent and athletics would finally reach the highest plateau of exposure—a game at home every time.

SPORTS

Don't Trade Players, Trade Whole Team

By PAUL T. OWENS

THE modern sports era has done everything but make everyone a winner. With all the billions spent on sports each year, the athletic establishment still has not discovered a way to keep the same team from losing often. There still is no guarantee that each fan in his or her sports lifetime will live in a winning town, during a winning season.

Losing ticket-holders pay only to be entertained by those who do not have what it takes to bring in the victory. Public competition is for communal thrills, the wonder and surprise of sport, but it goes too far if it is possible for any team or group of fans to be losers too often.

Winning has got to be distributed more evenly for American sports to truly be recognized as a just and equitable business enterprise. Losing fans that like to lose do not realize the masochism involved and can only turn to the system to help them change their image.

Stuck in a Losing Generation

League officials often change their rules so that the defense or offense will not dominate the game. Coaches can be fired and players traded and drafted in the name of better winning habits, but nothing is set up to bring a losing city a winner. If the fan does not move to a winning town, he could be stuck forever in another losing generation.

It should be mandatory for all teams to move regularly. The average life of a player in professional sports is close to five playing years. That is how long any team should stay in one city. Move in a winner and kick the loser out, if for nothing more than healthier sports veins flowing through the town.

A team with a record under .500 would move to a city that had a team over .500. The whole team goes. The players, owners, and team personnel. The league would conduct surveys to have an idea where the losers wanted to go. The fans also would have their say

Robert Neubecker

and vote from the list for their coming winner. It will be the only way they can fight aainst the cheap spending habits of team management and misguided draft choices.

These built-in franchise movements will add another dimension to any sport. The full impact of a love-hate relationship can be felt by everyone.

The player who hit the game-winning home runs last season against us will now be hitting them for us. The defensive back who intercepted six passes against us in one game last year will now be catching them and running the ball back for us. The defenseman in hockey at whom we yelled for beating up our players will now get our cheers when he starts his fights in our behalf.

121

SPORTS

DON'T TRADE PLAYERS, TRADE WHOLE TEAM

The modern sports era has done everything but make everyone a winner. With all the billions spent on sports each year, the athletic establishment still hasn't discovered a way to keep the same city team from losing too long. There still is no guarantee that each fan in his or her sports lifetime will live in a winning town, during a winning season. Losing ticket holders pay only to be entertained by those who don't have what it takes to bring in the victory. Public competition is for communal thrills, the wonder and surprise of sport, but it goes too far if it is possible for any team or group of fans to be losers too often.

Winning has got to be distributed more evenly for American sports to truly be recognized as a just and equitable business enterprise. Losing fans don't fully realize the masochism involved and can only turn to the system to help them change their self-image.

League officials often change their rules so that the defense or offense won't dominate the game. Coaches can be fired, players traded and drafted in the name of better winning habits; but nothing is set up to bring a losing city a winner. If the fan doesn't move to a winning town, he could be stuck forever in another losing generation.

It should be mandatory for all teams to move regularly. The average life of a player in professional sport is how long any team should stay in one city. Move in a winner and kick the loser out, if for nothing more than healthier sports veins flowing through the town. A team with a record under .500 would move to a city that had a team over .500. The whole team goes. The players, owners, and team personnel. The league would conduct surveys to have an idea where the losers wanted to go. The fans, also, would have their say and vote from the list for their coming winner. It will be the only way they can fight against the cheap spending habits of team management and misguided draft choices and trades.

These built-in franchise movements will add another dimension to any sport. The full impact of a love-hate relationship can be felt by everyone. The player who hit the game-winning home runs last season against us will now be hitting them for us. The defensive back who intercepted six passes against us in one game last year will now be catching them and running them back for us. The defenseman in hockey who we yelled at for beating up our players, will now get our cheers when he starts his fights in our behalf. Some fans will have some reservations about rooting for a player they have jeered so long, even if he is at the free-throw line about to sink the game-winning basket in the deciding championship game. The hope is, however, that the intense desire to win will overcome any possible psychological and emotional reservations.

The cost of moving teams will be added onto the price of game tickets. An overpriced end-zone seat won't look so bad when a losing fan realizes that next year a winner will be scoring most of the points right before his binoculared eyes. Team strategies would definitely be affected by the exchange of teams. During last minute negotiations, team general managers would be telling each other, "Based on the fact that we will have Cleveland's first round draft pick next year, and we will be playing in Pittsburgh, we can't afford to trade you our back-up center for your No. 1 shooting guard, 3rd string kick-off return specialist and the second cheerleader from the left."

The franchise moves could be protested, but the final vote of the Committee on the Equitable Disbursements of Winning Spirits would rule. If a city's mayor threatened a fan boycott and an injunction against the league from sending what he called the dirtiest team in the specter of sports, the committee could take away the right for anyone to bring any team to that city or within a 75-mile radius of it. The league's highest purpose is for spreading winning wealth to the largest number possible.

There will be no commiseration, though, from the rest of the sports world, for an ex-winning city when its people awaken to the first day of the exhibition season and the losing currents of their new team. The Los Angeles Giants. The Pittsburgh Falcons. The Houston Lions, the Chicago Lakers, not to mention the Philadelphia Brewers.

Such a sports system could affect the political arena. Imagine a quarterback who has been a favorite in every city in which he has played during his 25-year career. He will have earned enough grass-roots support to run his next team from the White House lawn, as coach from the 2nd floor window.

SUPER BOWL—PLAYED AT HOME AND AWAY

One Super Bowl game is not enough. Two would be fair, and three would be ideal. Instead of one game to determine the Super Bowl winner, a total of points scored in two games would be a better indication of how well the teams played against each other. In the week following the National Football Conference and American Football Conference games, the two Super Bowl teams would play a full game on one of their home fields. The next week another game would be played in the other team's stadium. If there was a tie score—both games totaled—a third game would be played the following week, at a neutral site.

Fans should have the big game played at least once at home. Going to the Super Bowl is an expensive outing with plane rides, hotel and entertainment during the pre-game festivities, etc. At home the same ambiance is affordable, and with a two-or-three game Super Bowl the League makes more money.

The most frustrated fans and team are those who do not win the Super Bowl game. They are entitled to having the game played at home. With the earning of the Super Bowl game comes the right to turn over Super Bowl dollars in their own city.

This Super Bowl alternative eliminates any type of home team advantage that would occur when one of the playing team's fields is the Super Bowl designated place, or if one team is playing in a stadium close to their city. The venue switching from one stadium to another would add excitement and drama to the game. And, how could the League resist two stadiums filled instead of one? Two games!! Maybe three!!!

HONESTY AND SPEED WILL WIN MORE THAN GAMES

Football can improve its image and promote more excitement in the game with an emphasis on honesty and a few slight changes of the rules. The heroics of truth have yet to be fully expressed in football. When a player commits a foul, he does not admit it. When he doesn't, every kid who sees the unadmitted foul can think, "Look, he gets away with things, so can I." The game loses its potential for moral instruction. Athletes can sell us everything but the dignity of admitting our mistakes.

There is a way of influencing the player to be openly honest. A reward. If he admits the infraction before an official throws a flag, the penalty will be reduced. Instead of fifteen yards marched off against his team, only ten. If a player admits a foul that the officials did not see, the team will be rewarded extra yardage or an extra down at another time during the game. The kid in the stands can count the times his favorite player admitted his mistakes and be prouder about that than if his team wins.

Time has kept the game from moving faster. A team is allowed thirty seconds to put the ball in play. What if it is not needed on certain plays? Couldn't the unused time accumulate and be credited to downs when the team wants to run down the clock? Wouldn't it be better to see quicker lining up for the snap than to wade through four quarters of thirty seconds allowed to put the ball in play each time?

The turnover creates excitement. The change in momentum can stimulate the adrenalin of the fan, giving new hope. But wouldn't it be even more exciting and important if there was an option called TURNOVER PLUS. This would allow the team that had intercepted a pass or recovered a fumble to add twenty yards to the return. One PLUS would be allowed during each half, but no part of the twenty yards could be used to get the ball into the end zone.

126

Downs! We have had enough of four downs. Every time it's four downs. Aren't we entitled to some variety in the set-up? What about five downs? What about descending numbers of downs? The first time the team gets the ball it has five downs to make ten yards. The second time it has possession it gets four downs, the third time three downs, etc. One set of two downs with only five yards to make a first could be included in the new variety of downs format. This would give the fan another dimension of the game to get excited about. They can anticipate, "Hey, if we have good field position with a 'five' we're in good shape." What will be the probability of coaches who love to run, running on the first down in a set of downs that has only one?

The kicking game could also do with some changes to affect new strategies. The placement of the goal posts, their width and height, have all been altered throughout history, but nothing has been done to give points based on from where the kick is made. A field goal attempted from within the first ten yards would score one point, within the next ten yards, two points and so on until the last ten yards of the field from where ten points would be given for completion. No more the automatic three-point try. The same thing for the extra point. We are tired of this being one point every time. Let the scoring team get additional points similar to the new field goal scoring for its "try after'" success. A team behind 9-6 with three seconds left, having just scored a touchdown can win the game with an extra point made from forty yards out.

Instead of punting from deep in their own territory, as a new strategy, the team can place the ball once each half at the regular kick-off line and surrender it from there in regular kick-off formation. Why not?

SECOND PLACE: THE DREADED MEDAL

The first Olympic victory is being able to participate in the Olympic Games. The second is winning a gold medal. But of the glory given to those achieving Olympic excellence, ironically, the least goes to the one closest to the gold—the silver medalist.

The world always wants to know what it means to be the winner. But what about the second-place finisher? Silver medalists are asked only who finished first and why they didn't win. For this reason the feelings of the athlete who finishes second are perhaps more interesting than the mere fact of gold or silver. The 1932 Olympic Games 100-meter hurdles event for women was won by Babe Didrikson (USA) in the Olympic and world-record time of 11.7. In second place with the exact same time was Evelyn Hall (USA). According to rules at that time, the decision about placements was made by on-track judges. But the closeness of the race made it controversial.

"If I thought I had been beaten," reminisced Evelyn Hall, "it wouldn't have been so difficult to live with second place all these years. But since I always felt I won or at least tied the race, it has not been easy to answer the thousands of questions about why I didn't win. When I show people the pictures they stop asking, but over 50 years of having to qualify that race has taken its toll on me."

There are millions of words written about the winners and hardly any about the other finishers. Those in second place have to face the harshest truth—they were the closest to winning, but didn't. Barbara Ferrell (USA) placed second in the 100-meter dash in the 1968 Olympic Games. "You have beaten everyone in the world except one person, but you feel like the entire world has beaten you. When I came back from Mexico City, it was as if I had never gone. No one wants to claim you when you're second place. The gold medal winners were being paraded all around. I was unclaimed by everyone but my coach. The rest of your life you have to answer for that."

Wayne Collett (USA) was the silver medalist in the 400-meter run at the 1972 Olympic Games in Munich. "Anything," says Collett, "would have been good enough, but second place?"

"Before I competed in the Games, another athlete on the Olympic team asked me how I would feel if I won. I replied, 'I would feel relieved.' He then asked how I would feel if I placed second. I replied, 'I would be disappointed and distressed.' He asked how I would feel if I won the bronze medal. I replied, 'I would feel as if I had accomplished a great deal in my sport.' I find this perspective a curious thing, but nonetheless I feel I might have been better off if I had won the bronze. Being in the Olympic Games and getting closer than anyone else to winning the gold medal, leaves a lot of questions unanswered."

But four-time gold medalist John Naber (USA) is as proud of his silver medal in the 200-meter freestyle than he is of the four gold medals he won as a backstroke competitor. His second-place finish in the 1976 Montreal Olympics was his best time in the event. It was also faster than the existing world record. "I was predicted to win the gold medals. In the 200-meter freestyle I went faster than what was considered my potential. That meant as much to me as my gold medals."

And silver isn't always bad—second place made a hero out of Lance Larson. In the 1960 Olympic 100-meter freestyle event, he finished with the best clocked time. The "visual" judges, however, were divided, and the chief judge broke the tie, giving the race to John Devitt (AUS). The public was outraged. Injustice was claimed. Larson, who was also a member of the freestyle relay gold-medal team, felt, "That with all the controversy over the freestyle race, it was as if I had won two gold medals. The Games are to give recognition. Not winning is what I am remembered for. People remember that more than if I had actually won the gold medal."

Many athletes have even learned to love second place. Mack Robinson (USA) took second to one of the greatest Olympians ever, Jesse Owens (USA), in the 200-meter dash of the 1936 Olympic

Games. "It was fantastic because you cannot get any closer. I tell people who want to know why I didn't win that there's just as much gold in my silver medal as there is in the gold. There is nothing you can discredit about second place. The only letdown is that the general public does not fully appreciate what the silver medalist has accomplished."

Shirley Babashoff (USA), swimmer in the 1972 and 1976 Games, is one of the greatest swimmers of all time. Of her total eight medals, six of them are silver. "The press and public had more trouble accepting my second-place medals than I did. I felt sorry for them, because they could not deal with it and wanted to put me down for not winning gold medals. They did not know what it was like to have worked like I did. They would remark after each race, 'Well, you got another silver,' and I would answer, 'It was my best effort. It was my best time. What more do I want?' The silver is fine with me. I am proud of every one of them."

Second place has also been a great motivator. Milt Campbell (USA) was gold medalist in the 1956 decathlon. He describes his silver-medal finish in the 1952 Olympic Games as "joy and elation. All I wanted to do was be on the Olympic team, but after I let second place set in, all I wanted to do was concentrate on winning the gold medal the next time. Second place was like finishing tenth. If I had finished tenth, I don't think it would have made that much of an impact on me, but since I had been second, my commitment to winning became the most important thing in my life. It became life and death. If I didn't win in 1956, I wasn't coming back."

If records are ever kept of second-place accomplishment, a few special instances in Olympic history would have to be included. Two involve the shortest time as a second-place winner, and another is for the longest wait to become second. The most spectacular reversal of seconds in Olympic history was, without doubt, in the 1928 Games. The band playing at the awards ceremony of the men's high diving contest was interrupted as the medals were being presented.

There had been an error in the scoring calculations, and the seeming gold-medal winner had to change places with the man who had been designated for the silver medal. Farid Simaika (EGY) won the silver medal after first being declared the winner. Pete Desjardins (USA) was then elevated to the first-place platform, setting the record for the shortest time in Olympic history standing on the second place platform.

In 1948, the silver medal in the 4X100-meter relay was awarded to the Italian team. During the presentation of the medals, the International Jury of Appeal received protests and, after re-examining the photos, decided to reinstate the disqualified American team for the gold medal. The Italians were given the third-place position, while the British team, originally designated the winners, was awarded the second-place position.

Ingemar Johansson (SWE) was a light heavyweight boxer in the 1952 Olympic Games but was disqualified in the finals of the event. Thirty years later his disqualification was overruled, and he was given his silver medal and second-place status.

But who really wants to be second place? No competitor goes into the competition wanting to come away with the silver medal. It still remains the most unwanted prize in any athletic competition. One competitor said, "I keep my gold and bronze medals and throw my silvers away. They remind me that I wasn't first." Although it has not always been a curse, Fred Delaney (USA), the 1948 shotput silver medalist, sums up the second place position the most accurately. "When you're so close, it's the gold that counts." But think of it—if there wasn't a second place, no one could say they won the gold.

BASKETBALL MUST TAKE A SHOT AT THE FUTURE

It's not the thirty-second clock or the high price of seats for high-priced talent, nor is it that the game's purpose of bouncing a leather ball up and down a polished wooden floor needs to be changed. But a futuristic facelift is needed for basketball to endure.

Without having to expand the court to accommodate increase in body size of the players, we can revolutionize the sport to everyone's benefit. While some critics of the game want the basket raised, and a few would like it lowered so no one has any leaping advantage, all that is really needed is a moving basket. One that goes up and down in a slow progression. The scoring target has been static too long.

Other sports have wider goal space, why not basketball? And not by increasing the size of the hoop, but by having two more baskets, one on each side of the center basket. Three points for a shot in the middle basket, two points for success on the sides. With the middle moving at all times, it would not always be the automatic target.

And, if a team recovers the ball in its back court, it will have four seconds--not ten--to get it into the front court.

What is so sacred about five players against five players? Why not have part of one quarter played with different numbers: three on three, four on four, two on two. Even have two games going on at once: while one side of the court goes three on three, the other is playing two on two.

There are elements of play and performance that should count on the scoreboard, points for teamwork and beautiful moves. For instance, if a team passes the ball a certain number of times before shooting a basket, it gets an extra point.

If any player makes a beautiful move, he should be awarded points for his team. A judge should be on the sidelines, like in a gymnastic performance, giving numerical credit for the aesthetics given to the game by its players. "Awe" inspiring moves will be judged as beauty points and added onto the totals as basketball is a gymnastic ballet, a dance with a bounce and a very soft touch. And the moves don't have to be followed by a completed basket. Effort and choreography need to show up on the point totals—even though the ball never went through the basket, and the guy from the other team has the rebound. Point of difficulty in shot selection should also be considered when determining how many points should be given for each made shot. Great defense, phenomenal control in mid air, and displays of expansive beauty--right out of the realm of what we thought was impossible--definitely have a place in scoring. A judge at courtside will add points to the game for the excessive grace performed, just like his fault-finding, foul-minded counterpart referee on the court blows whistles for all the negativity he sees.

Along with the sideline judges, one of the coaches on each team should be able to influence the game more than through screams of encouragement and exhorted commands. With an electronically controlled sixth man, the coaching staff will feel less of its usual helplessness in executing the intended game plan. With the use of one flex-plastic mannequin, the coaches will have an extra man to assist doing what the human players won't do or are unable to do. The only rule will be that the sixth men cannot guard each other. They will be used specifically for double teaming, light posting, and taking another player's concentration away. Their biggest asset to the game will be how well they can reduce the tension from playing the games from the bench.

With new ways to score, and new players on the court to watch, new speeds and strategies to understand, the game will get closer to its final evolutionary stage, when every player is playing by himself with his own basket--his left hand trying to score, while his right hand is trying to block the shot.

PROTECT YOUR LOCAL QUARTERBACK

The easiest way to protect your quarterback is to have him wear an airbag uniform that expands on contact. There are, however, less extreme ways for him to survive a game without being beaten by injuries.

If the quarterback signals to the defense that he will not stay in the pocket, he should be given a few free seconds before the rush to him begins. To balance this protective advantage, one receiver would be ineligible to catch the pass. And that receiver would have to be announced to the defense when he makes his signal.

On plays where he scrambles, give him credit for not being tackled. If he can keep away from the defense for five seconds, he is allowed five more of non-tackling aggression. After that he is fair game.

Let him have a safe place to operate. From anywhere beyond twenty yards behind the line of scrimmage he is free to roam untouched. All the defense can do in that space is chase him down, throw their hands up or fan placards in front of him to confuse him, but no tackling. As soon as he returns to an area inside the 'hitting' 20, go get him. To add some forward excitement to the game, if the defense does not down him after he runs past the first down mark, he can pass on the play.

We could eliminate a lot of pain and injury if only one or two players were allowed to tackle the quarterback. On every play the defense would have Designated Sackers, the only ones who can apply the final physical force. Everyone else who hits him pays. At the end of each quarter, accountants from each team will exchange checks signed by those who have abused the Two-Tackler-Only rule. The quarterbacks will get the monies directly from other players, which will reduce what teams have to pay them in salary. They get their wage for appearing on the field to play, and earn extras for being hit by the wrong man. Designated Sackers can be changed at any time during the game, but not during any play.

What about a set of downs that does not allow the hitting or tackling of the quarterback. Each quarter the offense can determine a time that they have the ball that no defensive player can knock down the quarterback. To stop any play all they have to do is touch him— And, lightly, too.

Why not play three quarterbacks in the backfield, and elimi- nate two positions on the line. Yes, one less set of linemen would give some new options for the defense to consider. No team wants its quarterbacks to become hard-hitting blockers in the backfield, but guard-converted quarterbacks could be in the game's future. The "halo" effect is another choice of protectionists, a five-yard circle always around the quarterback. A defensive player cannot be within that circle unless he is in the air. This will diffuse the impact when reaching the quarterbacks.

If not the airborne tackle, what about a cable that is attached to the quarterback from a control on the sidelines? Whenever the coaching staff thinks the defense should stop the pursuit for the sake of safety, the cable string will pick up the quarterback from the field, thereby stopping the play and the potential abuse.

With designer airbag inflatables, quarterbacks could sacrifice accuracy and mobility for their own survival. And instead of getting pleasure from sticking the quarterback into the ground, opposing players will feel lighter than air as they slide off the balloon-expanded uniform of the quarterback as he releases the ball and slips gently to the ground.

The New York Times

SPORTS

And Now a Few Vital Statistics About the Sport Fan

By PAUL T. OWENS

Most of us have been raised following some kind of sports average. Whether it was the batting average of a major league baseball player, how many yards our favorite football player carried the ball each time he ran or some other fact about a running, scoring and sweating hero, our thoughts were filled with numbers. In fact, so smart and accurate were we with all that we knew about sports that our parents wanted to know if we could trade it in for better grades in school.

We never developed though, a taste for statistics about the spectator, the fan who needs heroes and hot dogs to make sure he's still alive.

Let's take a look at Mrs. Fontella Lake. She was voted last year's Super Fan because she has not missed one baseball game in 14 years and has proved that she spends an average of 26.7 percent of her total family income on game tickets, hotdog dinners, sugar ice pop, cheering felt flags and autographed box scores.

Medical studies determined that she spends an average of 67.3 percent of her total personal energy discussing in loud terms with players, officials and friends the games she lives through. Mrs. Lake was selected by the players to be the No. 1 Mother Figure, for they have grown to expect her at every game and attribute a great part of their success to her spirited loyalty.

The team's most valuable player mentioned that she most typifies the major leagues as being the best place for big boys to play where their mothers know where they are. She will be escorted to every game this season in a limousine with five mannequins designed and dressed as her favorite players.

The average game has 305 fathers who promise their children that they'll be "right back" with the autographs of every player in the dugout, with an average of 304.5 returning with programs filled with signatures signed by themselves. The average father or mother chasing a foul ball for a souvenir bruises an average of 4.2 kids in the way.

Let Junior Do the Waiting

The average wait in line for hot dogs is 1.1 innings. The average wait in line for beer is just under two innings. The average for let-the-kid-wait-in-line for hot dogs and beer is almost three innings, with the last inning of that time spent by the father or mother looking for the kid.

Recyclable words and thoughts occur at the rate of 8.3 per person per minute in a crowd of less than 50,000 and extend to 13.9 a minute in a crowd num-

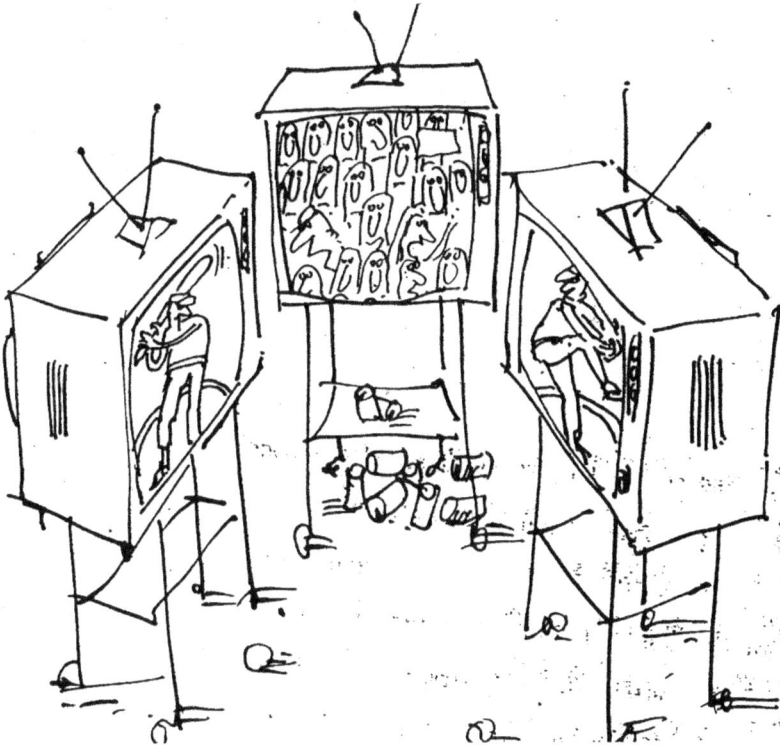

137

SPORTS

AND NOW A FEW VITAL STATISTICS
ABOUT THE SPORT FAN

Most of us have been raised following some kind of sports average. Whether it was the batting average of a major league baseball player; how many yards our favorite football player carried the ball each time he ran or some other fact about a running, scoring, and sweating hero, our thoughts were filled with numbers. In fact, so smart and accurate were we with all that we knew about sports that our parents wanted to know if we could trade it in for better grades in school.

We never developed, though, a taste for statistics about the spectator. The fan who needs heroes and hot dogs to make sure he's still alive. Let's take a look at Mrs. Sports Fan. She was voted last year's SUPER FAN because she has not missed one baseball game in fourteen years and has proven that she spends an average of 26.7% of her total family income on game tickets, hot dog dinners, sugar ice pop, cheering felt flags and autographed box scores.

It was determined by medical studies that she spends an average of 67.3% of her total personal energy discussing in loud terms with players, officials, and friends the games she lives through. Mrs. Sports Fan was selected by the players to be the Number One Mother Figure for they have grown to expect her at every game and attribute a great part of their success to her spirited loyalty. It was mentioned by the team's most valuable player that she most typifies the major leagues as being the best place for big boys to play where

138

their mothers know where they are. She will be escorted to every game this season in a limousine with five mannequins designed and dressed as her favorite players.

The average game probably has 305 fathers who promise their children that they'll be "right back" with the autographs of every player in the dugout, with an average of 304.5 returning with programs filled with signatures signed by themselves. The average father or mother chasing a foul ball for a souvenir bruises an average of 4.2 kids in the way. The average wait in line for hot dogs is 1.1 innings. The average wait in line for beer is just under 2 innings. The average let-the-kid-wait-in-line-hot-dog-and-beer line is almost 3 innings with the last inning of that time spent by the father or mother looking for the kid.

Recyclable words and thoughts occur at the rate of 8.3 per person per minute in a crowd of under 50,000 and extend to 13.9 per minute in a crowd numbering up to 125,000 people. The average sentence length in any game is 1.5 words. The longest sentence has lasted three innings. The average adult vocabulary decreases 25,000 words per game to sounds and words of 2.5 syllables or less.

The shortest temper was that of Alan B., age 59, who jumped onto the field after a center fielder missed two fly balls in one inning, grabbed the player's mitt and told him to get up in the stands, that he would finish the game for him.

The average fan injury starts at a picnic, from the bottle of beer that swims across the chest of America's afternoon of the fan trying to imitate the touchdown runner, and ends up around a lawn sprinkler with a twisted ankle.

The average crude fan interferes at least 3.7 times with every-one else's good time, throwing debris, obscenities and blocking views with their coarse physical personalities. Spilling 1.9 cups of coffee, coke, or beer down someone's shirt or shoes or on top of someone's head is included in their act.

The average fan running with his box of coffee and drinks and peanuts and popcorn to get to his seat in time for the kickoff has almost zero respect for those in his way. Fifty-eight per cent of all fans leave from 10 to 25 minutes before the game will end because they feel they know who the winner and loser will be. Less than 10 per cent of the sports audience will wait for twenty minutes after a game to allow the parking lots to empty to have less of a freeway-hugging bumper-to-bumper ride home.

The biggest exaggeration during the week happens in a barber shop where men who didn't go to the game boast about what happened based on what they have read in the newspaper or heard on the radio, and argue how they couldn't be wrong because, "I was there. I saw it. Now how can you argue?"

The average time spent reading the sports section for the average fan is 15 hours per week. The first thing people ask when they see you have a paper is if they can look at the sports section and when they say they'll return it, you, the average fan will tell them, "It's all right. I've already read it twice."

No matter if the average kid grows up to be a winner or loser, or neither, every one of them will have the question to ask each other on any Monday, "Hey, did you see what happened on Sunday?"

SPORT SOUNDS THAT CAN HEAL

I am looking for sports to provide more than just loving a winning town, a winning team, in a winning season.

Poets and historians have created and verified myths about ancient Greek athletes. Scientists have searched for genetic links between great athletes of today and thousands of years ago. But the sports enthusiasts have only gotten a fast view of excitement and a sudden call for the game to end and to go back to work again. Nothing has been done with the enormous power of enthusiasm generated by fans and athletes during sporting events. We haven't found a positive use or storage place for the energy and sound of human competition, the intensity of language, the guttural emotional release. They could be used to fight diseases.

Machinery must be devised to convert the hysteria of a football, basketball, baseball or hockey game into doses of therapeutic medicine. Bodies reconstituted by massive transfusions of tumult from the cheering crowds. Aging curtailed by the strength of play, of the urgency and sensitivity from the roaring masses. The sports section will testify that the healing spirit is at work:

NEW TREATMENT FOR KIDNEY STONES! Cured by the sheer force of sound from the football game between the Pittsburgh Steelers and the Denver Broncos.

ARTERIES THOROUGHLY CLEANSED! Arteries have unhardened from the roars at the hockey game between the Philadelphia Flyers and the Los Angeles Kings.

We'll be able to see these miracles taking place. As the scores of all games are announced, a monitor at the stadium and on the T.V. screen will show the medical benefits of the thunderous vibrations of losing and winning spirits.

This new energy will be tapped from all possible sources. Equipment will be attached to family television sets to absorb the energy from millions of dens and living rooms and transmitted to hospital patients. And business offices will broadcast the sounds of crowds at games for workers to improve their professional morale.

SPORTS

Some Loopholes for the Overtaxed Sports Fan

By PAUL T. OWENS

In this week of tribute to the tax collector, the average fan in the average sports-foaming city deserves a tax break. The fan who spends his days of rest "at work," emotionally supporting his team; the fan who celebrates every weekend gazing through end-zone binoculars; the fan who looks down a kaleidoscopic television tube at the

concept of Anticipatory Rebate.

The fanatic fan who considers himself so much a part of the team family that he goes to every away game can deduct traveling expenses, plastic buttons, felt hats, sun visors, earmuffs with radio attachments, and portable television units whose frequency spans all stadiums where the games that affect his team's league standing are being played. When the fan stays at home on an occasional Sunday, all electricity to keep the game on will

Arnie Ten

SPORTS

SOME LOOPHOLES FOR THE OVERTAXED SPORTS FAN

The average fan in the average sports-foaming city deserves a tax break. The fan who spends his days of rest "at work," emotionally supporting his team; the fan who celebrates every weekend gazing through end-zone binoculars; the fan who looks down a kaleidoscopic television tube at the possible pieces of his marriage —each fan is more than ready to have his emotional expenditure quantified in terms of money and put into the Internal Revenue Service form under the occupation of Fan.

Let's see what a new tax page might look like. After the fan states his home team (one per lifetime), he can profit from all emotional loopholes of a sports-watching life. If he goes to a game and his team loses, he should deduct the price of admission because he wasn't allowed to identify with a winner. If he suffers excessive emotional deprivation from that defeat or a losing season, additional deductions will be given.

The new tax form will apply to winning and losing. The cost of winning-game tickets and a possible surtax for excessive joy and happiness will be recorded on the tax page under Emotional Capital Gains. In a city whose team is dull and lethargic and a winner, the fan can deduct a nominal amount for Negative and Unfun Playing Services, based on the Federal athletic statue that asserts that Winning Isn't Everything. The fan can deduct half the ticket price if his team beats an "honest and reasonable" point spread, whether the team wins or loses.

If a fan has purchased tickets assuming that specific players will be on the team, and those players don't play (traded, etc.), the fan can deduct the price of tickets under the sports-tax concept of Anticipatory Rebate.

The fanatic fan who considers himself so much a part of the team family that he goes to every away game can deduct traveling expenses, plastic buttons, felt hats, sun visors, earmuffs with radio attachments, and portable television units whose frequency spans all stadiums where the games that affect his team's league standing are being played. When the fan stays at home on an occasional Sunday, all electricity to keep the game on will be paid for by the commercial sponsors, if he can prove the volume was as loud during the commercials as during the game.

When team owners negotiate for players from other teams, fans can donate land, stock and money to escalate the bidding price. All such gifts are tax deductible as Gifts for the Betterment of Municipal Morale.

The fan who refrains from booing or inciting violence will be compensated for Compassion for Overpaid Mistakes and Increase of Human Decency. If a fan detects officiating mistakes that are upheld by instant replay, he will receive gift certificates from the league involved to purchase official "booing" and "negative" white-striped leisure wear. Furthermore, he can deduct half the cost of psychotherapy if he considers his screaming enthusiasms at a game as therapeutic as an all-out self-analysis therapy session. Games in which a fan feels he could have played better than the players should be documented in game programs and turned in with the IRS form. If the fan's claims to superior skill convince the athletic tax authorities, he will receive free or discounted tickets to future games and may deduct the amount from his gross income.

Fans who feel they can change a team's losing ways will have halftime tryouts twice a season to prove their skills. And any time they show they can play better than a player, they will receive an invitation from the team to play in any 10 games they choose. If they decline to play, they may deduct the per-game salary equivalent of the player they can "outplay."

In short, the average fan needs a break. Especially the fan who doesn't have a business he can use to deduct tickets as a business expense. The fan whose business is the team. The team he loves and loves to hate. The team he would like to outgrow, but can't.

This fan is entitled to more than a throwaway bag of peanuts for all he has given to the game and his team. The team that belongs to him as much as to the team owners, the people who appreciate their incomes by depreciating the lives of athletic heroes. The fan who wears his own uniform with his number on his back. The number that specifies the number of dollars he has deducted from the "luxury" of defeat or the total he has added on for winning the game and the season.

CREDITS

Pictures courtesy of:
    LPI/LA 84 Foundation
    LA 84 Foundation
    Symes Photography
    University of Southern California Athletic Department
    Richard Mackson, photographer
    Long Photography
    James Roark, photographer
    Los Angeles Lakers
    Don Chadez, photographer
    Walter Loos Photography
    Victor Awards—Joe Di Maggio 1991, 50th Year Celebration
            of his 56 game hitting streak.
                Executive Producer, David Z. Marmel

Books:
    Leaners Out of the Wind,
    by Claudia J. Sobel and Paul T. Owens
    Don't Hit Him, He's Dead by John McDonough
    and Paul T. Owens
    The Kicking Game by Paul T. Owens with
    Ben Agajanian, Tom Landry

Articles and Poems:
    New York Times
    1984 Los Angeles Olympic Organizing Committee
    Stars in Motion Magazine
    Final Report of the 1984 Olympic Games

Editing
    Jo Ellen Krumm

www.ingramcontent.com/pod-product-compliance
Lightning Source LLC
LaVergne TN
LVHW021504080426
835509LV00018B/2387